WILLIAMS·SONOMA

# Food Processor

## COOKBOOK

Recipes by Abby Mandel

Photography by Penina

**WILLIAMS-SONOMA**
Founder and Vice-Chairman: Chuck Williams
Book Buyer: Victoria Kalish

**WELDON OWEN INC.**
President: John Owen
Vice President and Publisher: Wendely Harvey
Chief Operating Officer: Larry Partington
Vice President International Sales: Stuart Laurence
Associate Publisher: Lisa Atwood
Managing Editor: Hannah Rahill
Project Editor: Sarah Lemas
Consulting Editor: Norman Kolpas
Copy Editor: Sharon Silva
Design: Kari Perin, Perin+Perin
Production Director: Stephanie Sherman
Production Manager: Jen Dalton
Food Stylist: Sandra Cook
Prop Stylist: Sara Slavin

In collaboration with Williams-Sonoma
3250 Van Ness, San Francisco, CA 94109

**A WELDON OWEN PRODUCTION**

Copyright © 1999 Weldon Owen Inc.
814 Montgomery St., San Francisco, CA 94133
All rights reserved, including the right of
reproduction in whole or in part in any form.

Library of Congress has cataloged the 1st edition
of this book as follows:

Mandel, Abby.
    Food processor / by Abby Mandel : photography
by Penina.
       p.  cm. - - (Williams-Sonoma cookware series)
    Includes index.
    ISBN 1-887451-12-9
    1. Food processor cookery.  I. Title.  II. Series.
TX840.F6M363   1999
641.5'89 - - dc21      97-28573  CIP
ISBN 1-892374-08-0

First printed in 1999
10  9  8  7  6  5  4  3  2  1

Production by Toppan Printing Co., (H.K.) Ltd.
Printed in China

*A Note on Weights and Measures:*
*All recipes include customary U.S. and metric*
*measurements. Metric conversions are based on*
*a standard developed for these books and have*
*been rounded off. Actual weights may vary.*

# CONTENTS

*In the early 1970s, physicist and inventor Carl Sontheimer was looking for a culinary gadget to import as a retirement hobby. On a trip to France, he saw the Robot-Coupe, an appliance used by professional chefs to speed food preparation. Sontheimer acquired import rights, designed his own improvements, and came up with a new name: Cuisinart.*

Introduced in 1973, the first Cuisinart food processor arrived just as people were beginning to develop a new passion for cooking and for entertaining at home. With its powerful motor and ingenious accessories, it made preparing food easier, quicker, neater, and more pleasurable. By decade's end, the machine was a huge success, and other manufacturers jumped on Sontheimer's bandwagon, introducing their own versions of the popular food chopping and puréeing device.

Today, processors are standard fixtures in our kitchens, and they come with more power, greater capacity, and more accessories than ever. Cooks can even buy mini processors (at right) for smaller-scale tasks—particularly chopping small quantities of ingredients—unsuited to most bigger machines.

Yet, in structure and function, food processors remain as simple

as ever. Most full-size models include a sturdy base containing a
powerful motor that turns a central
post. Over that post fits a see-
through plastic work bowl. Inside
the bowl, a variety of blades or cutting discs may be seated securely
on the post. A lid covers the bowl
and safely keeps the machine from
operating unless securely locked
in place. Rising from the lid, a feed
tube with removable pusher per-
mits the addition of ingredients
while the machine is working. On
some machines, the pusher assembly can be removed from the feed
tube, allowing for the introduction
of larger ingredients. Two switches
operate the processor: "on" allows
the machine to run continuously,
while "off-pulse" lets you turn the
motor on and off in quick, con-
trolled bursts.

Although simple, a food processor can intimidate the cook who
has never used one. Because it per-
forms many preparation tasks in
almost the blink of an eye, it re-
quires attentiveness and planning
to ensure not only that ingredients
are processed to the desired degree
and no further, but also that a
recipe comes together efficiently.
That is the reason behind this book.
On the six pages that follow, you'll
find explanations of all the standard food processor components

and instructions on how to use
them correctly. Spend a few minutes practicing these basic tech-
niques. Then, start working your
way through the collection of
delicious recipes, which will teach
you even more about how to make
the most of a food processor. Keep
one thing in mind, though: This
book is not a substitute for your
machine's owner's manual. Be
sure to read through that booklet
carefully and to follow its specific
guidelines, precautions, and necessary troubleshooting tips.

*A wide range of standard components and optional accessories enable your processor to perform almost any food preparation task with speed and ease.*

METAL BLADE | Two curved stainless-steel blades chop ingredients to any consistency desired; purée vegetables or fruits; make nut butters; prepare mayonnaise and sauces; and mix batters and doughs, including small quantities of bread dough. Use in conjunction with the "off-pulse" button when chopping.

SHREDDING DISC | Sharp-edged holes cut firm vegetables such as carrots, potatoes, and zucchini (courgettes), as well as most firm or semihard cheeses, into long, thin shreds. It can also cut nuts and chocolate into small bits. A medium-shred disc is a standard component; a fine shredder is an optional accessory.

SLICING DISC | Used in conjunction with the feed tube, the serrated edge of a standard slicing disc neatly cuts whole fruits, vegetables, cooked meat, partially frozen raw meat, and baguettes into slices 4 mm thick. Thick (6 mm), medium (3 mm), thin (2 mm), and ultrathin (1 mm) discs are also available.

DOUGH BLADE | The stubby, curved dual blades of this durable, all-plastic food processor component efficiently mix and knead larger quantities of yeast-leavened bread dough.

GRATING DISC | Optional disc has sharp, small rasps ideal for grating hard cheeses, chocolate, nuts, coconut, or ice into fine particles. Ingredients are fed to the grating disc via the feed tube.

CITRUS JUICER | Securely seated in a large sleeve (not pictured) on top of the food processor's work bowl, this optional attachment includes a power drive that reduces the motor speed to allow for the easy rotation of large, medium, or small cone attachments for reaming grapefruit, orange, or lemon halves. A rotating filter basket rids the extracted juice of seeds and pulp.

WHISK | Designed to connect to a processor's driveshaft, this optional device causes two stainless-steel whisks to whirl rapidly while the arm to which they are attached moves slowly around the perimeter of the work bowl. Ideal for whisking egg whites, sauces, and batters.

JULIENNE DISC | Optional discs cut firm vegetables into neat, long shreds that are perfectly square in cross section, as if cut by a chef's expert hand. Available in fine (2 mm) and medium (3 mm) sizes.

Metal Blade

Shredding Disc

Slicing Disc

Dough Blade

Grating Disc

Citrus Juicer

Whisk

Julienne Disc

*Made of stainless steel honed to a sharp, serrated edge, the metal blade is the most versatile food processor tool, capable of mincing, chopping, puréeing, or blending a wide range of ingredients. Because it is so sharp, it calls for extreme caution in handling. Follow all instructions carefully, and always pick up the metal blade by its plastic post.*

The three photographs and captions shown below and opposite illustrate the most basic uses of the metal blade: mincing, chopping, and puréeing. A few additional words of explanation will help you achieve excellent results with ease.

Most importantly, always take care to cut up larger ingredients by hand into uniform-sized pieces of about 1 inch (2.5 cm). This step ensures that the final mince or chop will be even and that purées will be smooth. Pay attention, too, to the guidelines given by the manufacturer in your particular model's instruction booklet for the maximum amount of food your model can safely and efficiently process at one time and do not exceed it.

### mincing

To mince small items, such as garlic cloves (at right) or shallots, insert the metal blade, secure the lid, and turn the machine on. Drop in the items through the feed tube and, when they reach a fine consistency, turn off the machine.

### chopping

Put the ingredients in the work bowl and secure the lid. Push the "off-pulse" switch on and off in 1-second bursts until the food is chopped as desired. Stop occasionally and remove the lid to check, using a rubber spatula to scrape down the sides of the work bowl, if necessary.

### puréeing

Put the ingredients in the work bowl and secure the lid. Using the "off-pulse" switch, turn the machine on and off several times to chop the ingredients coarsely. Stop and scrape down the work bowl. Then, using the "on" switch, turn the machine on and process until puréed.

All ingredients to be minced or chopped should be firm and dry. Overripe produce, particularly tomatoes, will turn into a purée if you try to chop them. Before chopping meat, poultry, or seafood, chill it well in the refrigerator. Don't attempt to process any cheese that is too hard to cut easily with a knife, as it can damage the metal blade or the processor motor.

When puréeing, it may take as long as 2 minutes for some foods to become smooth. This particularly holds true for transforming nuts into nut butters. You may also have to add a little liquid from the recipe to ease processing. And remember, you cannot use the metal blade to mash potatoes, which will become glutinous.

Before you process any food, always check to make sure that the metal blade is securely seated on the post in the center of the work bowl. If a chunk of food gets stuck between the blade and the side or bottom of the bowl, carefully lift out the blade by its plastic post and dislodge the food, keeping your fingers clear of the blade's sharp edges. Empty the bowl, return the blade, and secure the lid. Then turn on the machine and pour the ingredients back in through the feed tube. Finally, pay special attention whenever a recipe suggests that you stop and scrape down the work bowl. The ultrafast speed at which the blade turns flings food particles against the sides of the bowl. Use a plastic or rubber spatula to return these particles to the bottom of the bowl to ensure even processing.

*The dough blade is specifically designed for making bread dough. It quickly mixes together the dry ingredients and liquids, then its rapid rotation kneads the dough for you. It cannot, however, be used for very stiff doughs that would not be comfortably kneaded by hand.*

A few tips will help you achieve consistently good results when using the dough blade.

Check the capacity of your processor to make sure it can handle the amount of dough you are making.

If necessary, work in two or more batches. Always measure your ingredients carefully, following the recipe precisely.

Note, too, that the speed with which a processor mixes and kneads dough creates friction that raises the dough's temperature and could interfere with the activity of yeast. To keep temperatures from rising too high, make sure that all liquids you use are cold, except for the lukewarm (110°F/43°C) water used to dissolve the yeast.

### mixing

Insert the dough blade. Add all dry ingredients and any oil or solid fats. Secure the lid and process briefly to mix. Remove the pusher from the feed tube. With the machine on, gradually add the liquids, pouring only as fast as they can be absorbed by the dry ingredients.

### kneading

Continue adding liquids until a soft dough forms and becomes a ball that rides around the bowl on the blade. Then process for about 60 seconds to knead. To check if the dough is properly kneaded, stop the machine and touch the dough. It should feel soft, pliable, and slightly sticky.

### shredding

Insert the shredding disc and place the lid on the processor. Cut the ingredients into pieces as long as the width of the tube. Stack them on their sides in the tube, secure the pusher assembly on top, turn on the machine, and press down firmly to shred.

### slicing

Insert the slicing disc and secure the lid. Trim the ends of the ingredients flat, cutting them to a length that will fit inside the feed tube. Insert the ingredients, filling the tube snugly. Secure the pusher assembly, turn on the machine, and press down to slice.

*A food processor's standard cutting discs produce some of its most decorative effects: long shreds or neat slices. Your success in producing both depends upon careful advance preparation of ingredients.*

Always take care that the ingredients fit the feed tube. Smaller items such as apples, onions, or other round fruits or vegetables may be put in halved or, if quite small, whole; larger ingredients such as cucumbers should be cut into sections.

For the longest possible shreds, cut ingredients as long as the width of the tube, stacking them horizontally inside the tube like the carrots shown at top left. For neat, cross-sectional slices, trim the ends of ingredients absolutely flat, as shown with the zucchini (courgette) at bottom left, so that they will remain stable during processing.

Observe a few precautions when using either disc. While it is important to fill the feed tube snugly enough to process an ingredient properly, never pack the feed tube so full that it becomes hard to press down the pusher. Use light pressure for soft items, medium for most foods, and firm pressure, but not too hard, for hard vegetables. Finally, never put your fingers or a spatula in the feed tube while operating the machine.

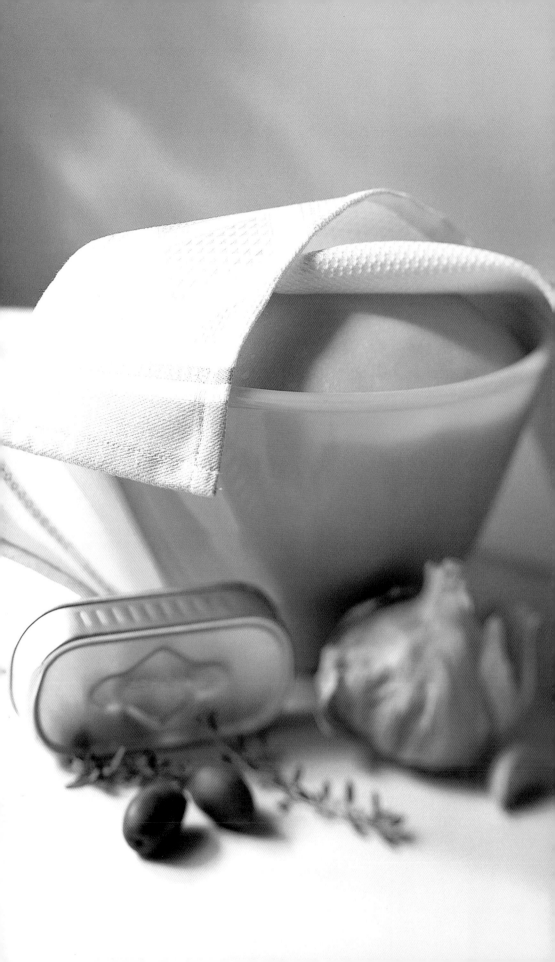

**STARTERS, SOUPS, AND BREADS**

# Goat Cheese Salsa Verde

SERVES 12

*This flavorful dip for crudités is inspired by the Italian* salsa verde. *Serve it with fennel wedges, small whole carrots, young radishes, red bell pepper (capsicum) strips, or any of your favorite seasonal vegetables.*

1 small clove garlic

1-inch (2.5-cm) cube yellow onion

1 cup (1 oz/30 g) fresh flat-leaf (Italian) parsley leaves

3 1/2-oz (105-g) piece fresh goat cheese, halved

1/4 cup (2 oz/60 g) light cream cheese

1/4 cup (2 fl oz/60 ml) light sour cream

1 teaspoon lemon juice

1 tablespoon extra-virgin olive oil

1 tablespoon capers

1/2 teaspoon anchovy paste

ground pepper to taste

Using the metal blade, turn the processor on and drop the garlic through the feed tube. Process until finely minced. With the processor still on, drop in the onion and process until finely minced. Turn off the processor. Add the parsley, goat cheese, cream cheese, and sour cream and process until smooth.

Using a rubber spatula, scrape down the work bowl and add the lemon juice, olive oil, capers, anchovy paste, and pepper. Process until well mixed. Transfer to a bowl and serve. (Or cover and refrigerate for up to 1 day. Stir well, adjust the seasonings, and bring to room temperature before serving.) ✳

# Italian Cheese Puffs

MAKES ABOUT 36 PUFFS; SERVES 12–16

*These bitefuls are an Italian version of French gougères,
Gruyère-flavored pastry puffs. Because they freeze and reheat well,
they're great to have on hand for unexpected guests.*

2-oz (60-g) piece Parmesan cheese, rind removed
and cut into 4 equal pieces, at room temperature

2-oz (60-g) piece pecorino cheese, rind removed
and cut into 4 equal pieces, at room temperature

1 large clove garlic

$^1/_2$ cup (4 oz/125 g) unsalted butter

$^1/_4$ teaspoon red pepper flakes

1 $^1/_2$ teaspoons dried oregano

1 cup (8 fl oz/250 ml) club soda or water

1 cup (5 oz/155 g) all-purpose (plain) flour

4 eggs

1 egg whisked with $^1/_2$ teaspoon salt for glaze

Position 2 racks in the middle of an oven and preheat to 400°F
(200°C). Butter 2 baking sheets. Sprinkle them with water and
shake off the excess. (The steam that develops during baking
keeps the puffs from sticking to the pan.)

Using the metal blade, pulse the Parmesan cheese to break it
up. Then process until minced. Transfer to a bowl. Repeat with
the pecorino cheese. Add to the Parmesan. Set aside.

Turn the processor on and drop the garlic through the feed tube.
Process until finely minced.

In a small saucepan over medium heat, melt the butter. Add the
garlic, red pepper flakes, and oregano. Cook, stirring often, until
hot and fragrant, about 20 seconds. Add the club soda or water,
bring to a simmer, and remove from the heat. Using a wooden

spoon, beat in the flour until the mixture forms a mass and pulls away from the sides of the pan. Then cook over medium heat, stirring often, until a film forms on the bottom of the pan, about 1 minute.

Transfer the hot dough to the work bowl (it is not necessary to clean it). Let rest for 5 minutes. Turn the processor on. Add the eggs through the feed tube one at a time, processing until smooth. Add the minced Parmesan and pecorino cheeses and process until mixed.

Transfer the dough to a pastry (piping) bag fitted with a $1/2$-inch (12-mm) plain tip. Pipe out $1^1/2$-inch (4-cm) balls about 2 inches (5 cm) apart onto the prepared baking sheets. Using a fingertip, dab the glaze on the balls, smoothing out any uneven edges.

Bake until browned, about 22 minutes, switching pan positions halfway through baking. Turn off the oven and leave the puffs in the oven for 10 minutes. Transfer to a rack, let cool briefly, then serve. ✳

# Fresh Tomato and Basil Soup

SERVES 4 OR 5

*The processor minces the skins of the tomatoes so finely that
they are barely detectable in this refreshing soup. Stored in
the refrigerator overnight, it even improves in flavor.
Serve the soup chilled—as here—or warm over medium heat
to serve hot. Garnish with thinly sliced basil leaves and
slivers of red onion, if you like.*

2-inch (5-cm) cube red (Spanish) onion, halved

1/2 cup (1/2 oz/15 g) fresh basil leaves

2 lb (1 kg) ripe tomatoes, seeded and cut into
1-inch (2.5-cm) chunks

2 cups (16 fl oz/500 ml) tomato juice

1 1/2 tablespoons balsamic vinegar

1/2 teaspoon ground cumin

1/2 teaspoon sugar

1/2 teaspoon salt

cayenne pepper to taste

Using the metal blade, combine the onion and basil and process
until minced. Add the tomatoes and process until puréed, stopping once or twice to scrape down the sides of the work bowl.

Transfer the tomato mixture to a bowl. Add the tomato juice,
vinegar, cumin, sugar, salt, and cayenne pepper and stir well.
Taste and adjust the vinegar and other seasonings. Cover and
chill well, about 3 hours.

To serve, ladle into bowls. ✳

# Eggplant Soup
# with Red Pepper Swirl

SERVES 4–6

*The combination of onion, parsnip, and tahini (sesame seed paste) helps to balance any hint of bitterness in the eggplant. The soup and garnish can be made up to 2 days in advance and refrigerated, or they can be frozen separately for up to 1 month. The soup can also be served chilled.*

2 red bell peppers (capsicums)

2 tablespoons olive oil

$^1/_8$ teaspoon plus $^1/_4$ teaspoon salt

2 large cloves garlic

1 large yellow onion, cut into 1-inch (2.5-cm) chunks

1 eggplant (aubergine), peeled and cut into
1-inch (2.5-cm) chunks

1 parsnip, peeled and cut into 1-inch (2.5-cm) chunks

$2^1/_2$–3 cups (20–24 fl oz/625–750 ml) chicken broth

$^1/_2$ teaspoon ground cumin

pinch of red pepper flakes

$1^1/_2$ teaspoons tahini

$^1/_4$ cup (2 fl oz/60 ml) light sour cream

22

Preheat a broiler (griller). Cut off the bottom and sides of each bell pepper in flat slabs. Discard the tops and any seeds. Place the slabs, cut sides down, on an aluminum foil–lined baking sheet. Broil (grill) about 6 inches (15 cm) from the heat until the skins blacken and blister. Remove from the broiler and wrap the peppers loosely in the foil lining. When cool enough to handle, peel away the skins.

Using the metal blade, combine 1 of the roasted peppers, 1 table-spoon of the olive oil, and the $^1/_8$ teaspoon salt and purée until very smooth. Set aside for garnish. Wash the work bowl and metal blade.

Turn the processor on and drop the garlic through the feed tube. Process until finely minced. Add half of the onion chunks and pulse to chop coarsely.

In a saucepan over medium-high heat, warm the remaining 1 tablespoon olive oil. When hot, add the garlic and onion. Im-mediately add the remaining onion chunks to the processor and pulse to chop coarsely. Add to the saucepan, stir well, and cook, stirring often, until the onion has softened, about 4 minutes.

Meanwhile, add the eggplant to the processor and pulse to chop coarsely. Transfer to a bowl. Then add the parsnip to the proces-sor and pulse to chop coarsely.

When the onion is ready, add the eggplant, parsnip, $2^1/_2$ cups (20 fl oz/625 ml) of the broth, the remaining roasted pepper, the cumin, the $^1/_4$ teaspoon salt, and the red pepper flakes. Bring to a boil, cover, reduce the heat to medium-low, and simmer until all the vegetables are tender, about 20 minutes.

Pour the soup through a sieve placed over a bowl, reserving the liquid. Using the metal blade, combine the solids from the sieve, tahini, and sour cream and process until completely smooth. Turn the processor on and pour about 1 cup (8 fl oz/250 ml) of the reserved liquid through the feed tube, processing until smooth.

Return the purée to the saucepan with the remaining reserved liquid. Stir well and reheat gently over medium heat. Add the remaining $^1/_2$ cup (4 fl oz/125 ml) chicken broth if the soup is too thick. Taste and adjust the seasonings. Ladle into warmed soup bowls and garnish with the pepper purée. ✻

23

# Apricot Tea Bread

MAKES 1 LOAF

*For the best flavor, wrap this dense, sweet bread in plastic wrap and store at room temperature for a day or two before serving.*

<sup></sup>³/₄ cup (3 oz/90 g) walnuts

1 ¹/₄ cups (6¹/₂ oz/220 g) all-purpose (plain) flour

¹/₂ teaspoon salt

³/₄ cup (4¹/₂ oz/140 g) dried apricots

¹/₂ cup (4 fl oz/125 ml) hot water

1 teaspoon baking soda (bicarbonate of soda)

³/₄ cup (6 oz/185 g) sugar

3 tablespoons vegetable oil

1 egg

2 teaspoons vanilla extract (essence)

Preheat an oven to 350°F (180°C). Butter and flour an 8¹/₂-by-4¹/₂-by-2¹/₂-inch (21.5-by-11.5-by-6-cm) loaf pan. Tap out excess flour.

Using the metal blade, pulse the walnuts to chop coarsely. Transfer to a small bowl. Stir in the flour and salt. Set aside. Pulse the apricots until coarsely chopped. Transfer to another bowl. Add the hot water and baking soda and stir well. Set aside.

Combine the sugar, vegetable oil, egg, and vanilla in the work bowl and process until very smooth. Spoon the flour mixture evenly over the base mixture. Spoon the apricot mixture over the flour. Pulse until just mixed. Do not overprocess; the surface flour will be mixed into the batter as it is removed from the work bowl. Pour the batter into the prepared pan.

Bake until browned and a toothpick inserted into the center comes out clean, about 45 minutes. Remove from the oven and let rest in the pan on a rack for 10 minutes. Then invert the loaf onto the rack and lift off the pan. Let cool. Cut into thin slices to serve. ✳

# Garlic-Thyme Baguettes

MAKES 12 BAGUETTES; SERVES 12–16

*These slim loaves have a soft interior and a nice, crisp crust.*

### FOR THE GLAZE

1 egg

½ teaspoon salt

### FOR THE DOUGH

2 large cloves garlic

3 tablespoons olive oil

2 teaspoons dried thyme

1 package (2½ teaspoons) active dry yeast

1 teaspoon sugar

1⅓ cups (11 fl oz/340 ml) lukewarm water (110°F/43°C)

2½ cups (12½ oz/390 g) all-purpose (plain) flour,
plus flour as needed

2½ cups (12½ oz/390 g) bread flour

1¼ teaspoons salt

To make the glaze, using the metal blade, combine the egg and salt and process until mixed. Transfer to a small jar and refrigerate until needed. It is not necessary to wash the work bowl before continuing.

To make the dough, using the metal blade, turn the processor on and drop the garlic through the feed tube. Process until finely minced.

In a small frying pan over medium heat, warm 2 tablespoons of the olive oil. Add the garlic and thyme and sauté until fragrant, about 15 seconds. Remove from the heat.

In a small bowl, dissolve the yeast and sugar in the lukewarm water. Let stand until bubbles start to rise, about 10 minutes.

Using the dough or metal blade, combine the 2½ cups (12½ oz/390 g) all-purpose flour, the bread flour, the salt, and the garlic mixture and process to mix. Turn the processor on and slowly add the yeast mixture through the feed tube, processing until combined. Then add the remaining 1 tablespoon oil through the feed tube, processing until the mixture forms a ball and cleans the sides of the work bowl. If the dough is too wet, add more flour by the tablespoon. If the dough is too crumbly, add more water by the tablespoon. When the dough is quite moist but not sticking to the sides, process until uniformly supple and elastic.

Transfer the dough to a large plastic bag and squeeze out the air. Seal the bag and put it in a bowl. Let the dough rise in a warm place until doubled in bulk, about 1 hour.

Butter a double baguette pan. Punch down the dough and turn out onto a lightly floured work surface. Cut the dough in half. Roll out each half into a 4-by-15-inch (10-by-37.5-cm) rectangle. Roll up each rectangle into a 15-inch (37.5-cm) log, pinching the seams tightly to seal. Place, seam side down, in the prepared pan. Cover with oiled plastic wrap. Let rise until doubled in bulk, about 1 hour.

Preheat an oven to 400°F (200°C).

27

Using a serrated knife, make 3 diagonal slashes about $1/4$ inch (6 mm) deep on each loaf. Lightly brush the glaze on the surface of the loaves.

Bake until browned and the loaves sound hollow when tapped on the bottom, about 25 minutes. Transfer to a rack to cool. Serve at room temperature. ❋

# Spinach Hummus

### SERVES 12–16

*Prepare a batch of this tangy hummus and spread it on garlic toasts or warm crisp pita triangles. Thinned with water, it is a great dip for crudités. In either case, it can be made ahead and refrigerated overnight or frozen for up to 1 month. Bring to room temperature, stir well, and adjust the seasonings before serving.*

3 large cloves garlic

2 cans (14½ oz/455 g each) chickpeas (garbanzo beans), rinsed and well drained

1 cup (1½ oz/45 g) firmly packed baby spinach leaves

2 tablespoons tahini

⅓ cup (3 fl oz/80 ml) lemon juice

2 teaspoons ground cumin

1 teaspoon salt

ground pepper to taste

½ cup (4 fl oz/125 ml) extra-virgin olive oil

Using the metal blade, turn the processor on and drop the garlic through the feed tube. Process until finely minced. Turn off the processor. Put the chickpeas, spinach, tahini, lemon juice, cumin, salt, and pepper in the work bowl and process until smooth. Turn off the processor and scrape down the sides of the work bowl. With the processor on, slowly pour the olive oil through the feed tube and process until smooth. Taste and adjust the seasonings.

Transfer to a bowl and serve. ✳

# Provençal Pizza

### SERVES 6–8

*This recipe yields enough dough for two 11-inch (28-cm) pizzas. Roll out the second crust, wrap airtight, and freeze for up to 1 month, then thaw, top, and bake when you want pizza in a hurry.*

**FOR THE DOUGH**

1 package (2½ teaspoons) active dry yeast

1 teaspoon sugar

1 cup (8 fl oz/250 ml) plus 1 tablespoon lukewarm water (110°F/43°C), plus water as needed

3¼ cups (16½ oz/515 g) all-purpose (plain) flour, plus flour as needed

1½ teaspoons salt

2 tablespoons olive oil

**FOR THE TOPPING**

6-oz (185-g) piece chilled Gruyère cheese, halved

1 large clove garlic

2 large yellow onions, quartered lengthwise

2 tablespoons plus 1 teaspoon extra-virgin olive oil

⅔ cup (5 fl oz/160 ml) water

1 tablespoon packed fresh thyme leaves

¾ teaspoon salt

ground pepper to taste

scant 1 tablespoon Dijon mustard

1 can (2 oz/60 g) anchovy fillets in olive oil, drained, blotted, and split lengthwise

16 Niçoise olives, pitted and halved, or 8 Kalamata olives, pitted and cut into narrow strips

For the dough, in a small bowl, dissolve the yeast and sugar in the lukewarm water. Let stand until bubbly, about 5 minutes.

Using the dough or metal blade, combine the 3¼ cups (16½ oz/ 515 g) flour and the salt and process to mix. Turn the processor on and slowly add the yeast mixture through the feed tube, processing until combined. Then add the oil through the feed tube, processing until the mixture forms a ball and cleans the sides of the work bowl. Mix in more flour or water to achieve the desired consistency. When the dough is quite moist but not sticking to the sides, process until uniformly supple and elastic.

Transfer the dough to an oiled bowl and turn to oil the top. Cover with a towel and let rise until doubled in bulk, about 1 hour.

Position a rack in the upper third of an oven and preheat to 400°F (200°C). Oil an 11-inch (28-cm) pizza pan.

Meanwhile, make the topping (do not wash the work bowl): Using the shredding disc, shred the cheese and transfer to a bowl. Using the metal blade, turn the processor on and drop the garlic through the feed tube. Process until finely minced. Leave in the work bowl. Using the slicing disc, stand the onion quarters in the feed tube and process to slice.

In a large, nonstick frying pan over medium heat, warm 1 tablespoon of the oil. Add the garlic, onions, water, thyme, salt, and pepper; stir well. Cover and cook, stirring often, until the onions soften, about 10 minutes. Uncover and cook, stirring occasionally, until the mixture begins to caramelize, about 12 minutes longer. Stir in 1 tablespoon of the oil. Remove from the heat. Taste and adjust the seasonings.

Punch down the dough and turn out onto a lightly floured work surface. Cut in half. Roll out each half into an 11-inch (28-cm) round. Wrap 1 round well and freeze for future use. Transfer the other to the prepared pan and spread with the mustard. Sprinkle with the cheese, then the onions. Arrange the anchovies and olives on top. Drizzle with the 1 teaspoon oil.

Bake until the edges are well browned, about 30 minutes. Remove from the oven and let rest for 10 minutes, then cut into wedges and serve warm. ✳

31

# Country Vegetable Soup with Pistou

**SERVES 8**

*Pair this hearty vegetable soup with a green salad, a wedge of cheese, and warm crusty bread for a satisfying supper. A dollop of pistou, the French cousin to Italian pesto, is stirred in at the table.*

**FOR THE PISTOU**

$1/4$-lb (125-g) piece Parmesan cheese

2 large cloves garlic

2 cups (2 oz/60 g) loosely packed fresh basil leaves

pinch of salt

$1/3$ cup (3 fl oz/80 ml) extra-virgin olive oil

2 large cloves garlic

2 leeks, white part and $1 1/2$ inches (4 cm) of green, cut into 1-inch (2.5-cm) pieces

2 slender carrots, peeled and halved

1 tablespoon olive oil

1 can (14$1/2$ oz/455 g) diced tomatoes with juice

1 can (15 oz/470 g) Great Northern or other small white beans, rinsed and well drained

$3 1/2$ cups (28 fl oz/875 ml) vegetable broth

3–4 cups (24–32 fl oz/750 ml–1 l) water

2 small zucchini (courgettes), cut into 1-inch (2.5-cm) pieces

1 cup (3 oz/90 g) broken capellini pasta

$1/2$ teaspoon salt

ground pepper to taste

$1/2$ lb (250 g) green beans, trimmed and cut into 1-inch (2.5-cm) lengths

$1 1/2$ cups (7$1/2$ oz/235 g) shelled peas

red pepper flakes

To make the *pistou,* using a sharp knife, trim the rind from the cheese and reserve. Cut the cheese into 3 equal pieces. Using the metal blade, pulse the cheese to break it up. Then process until finely minced. Add the garlic cloves, basil, and salt and process to mince. With the processor on, slowly pour the olive oil through the feed tube and process until smooth. Scrape into a bowl and set aside.

Using the metal blade, turn the processor on and drop the garlic through the feed tube. Process until finely minced. Turn off the processor. Put the leeks in the work bowl and pulse to chop coarsely. Transfer to a bowl. Using the slicing disc, stand the carrots in the feed tube and process to slice; set aside.

In a heavy nonaluminum saucepan over medium-high heat, warm the olive oil. Add the garlic and leeks and cook uncovered, stirring often, until the leeks soften, about 4 minutes. Add the carrots, tomatoes with juice, Great Northern beans, vegetable broth, 3 cups (24 fl oz/750 ml) of the water, and the reserved cheese rind. Simmer uncovered, stirring occasionally, for 20 minutes.

33

Using the metal blade, pulse half the zucchini pieces to chop coarsely. Add to the pot. Repeat with the remaining zucchini and add to the pot with the pasta, salt, and pepper. Simmer uncovered, stirring often, about 10 minutes longer.

Add the green beans and simmer for 5 minutes. Add the peas and simmer until the green beans are tender, 3–5 minutes longer. If the soup is too thick, thin with as much of the remaining 1 cup (8 fl oz/250 ml) water as needed. Taste and adjust the seasonings.

Ladle into warmed bowls and serve. Pass the *pistou* and red pepper flakes at the table. ✳

SALADS AND SIDE DISHES

# Thai Cabbage Slaw

## SERVES 6

*This slaw develops the perfect flavor balance when it's made
a day ahead. Cover and refrigerate until ready to serve.*

### FOR THE DRESSING

1/3 cup (1/3 oz/10 g) fresh cilantro (fresh coriander) leaves

1/2 red (Spanish) onion, quartered

1/4 cup (1 1/4 oz/37 g) lightly salted dry-roasted peanuts

1/3 cup (3 fl oz/80 ml) seasoned rice vinegar

2 tablespoons peanut oil

1 1/2 teaspoons fish sauce

1 teaspoon lemon juice·

1/4 teaspoon red pepper flakes

### FOR THE SLAW

3 carrots, peeled and cut into 4-inch (10-cm) lengths

1/2 medium-large head napa cabbage, cored
and cut to fit vertically in feed tube

1 red bell pepper (capsicum), seeded and finely diced

To make the dressing, using the metal blade, combine the cilantro,
onion, and peanuts and pulse to chop coarsely. Transfer to a
large bowl and add the rice vinegar, peanut oil, fish sauce, lemon
juice, and red pepper flakes. Stir to mix.

To make the slaw, using the shredding disc, lay the carrot pieces
in the feed tube and process to shred. Leave in the work bowl.
Using the slicing disc, stand the cabbage pieces in the feed tube
and process to slice. Add the carrots and cabbage to the dressing
along with the bell pepper. Toss to mix well. Cover tightly and
refrigerate until chilled, about 3 hours or for up to 1 day.

To serve, toss well, drain off any liquid, and taste and adjust the
seasonings. Serve chilled. ✳

# Warm Southwest Potato Salad

**SERVES 6**

*Raw corn kernels give this roasted potato salad some crunch.*

1 lb (500 g) small red potatoes (about 20), halved

2 tablespoons olive oil

1 teaspoon salt

2 ears of corn

1 clove garlic

1 jalapeño chile, seeded

1/2 small red (Spanish) onion, cut into thirds

1/2 cup (1/2 oz/15 g) fresh cilantro (fresh coriander) leaves

4 plum (Roma) tomatoes, quartered and seeded

1 tablespoon lime juice

38

Preheat an oven to 400°F (200°C).

Put the potatoes in a bowl. Add 1 tablespoon of the olive oil and 1/2 teaspoon of the salt and toss to mix. Spread the potatoes, cut sides down, in a shallow roasting pan. Reserve the bowl. Roast until just tender but not mushy, 25–30 minutes, stirring after 20 minutes.

Meanwhile, cut the kernels from the ears of corn and transfer to the bowl that held the potatoes.

Using the metal blade, turn the processor on and drop the garlic through the feed tube. Process until finely minced. Then drop the chile through the feed tube and process until finely minced. Add the onion, cilantro, and tomatoes and pulse to chop coarsely. Do not overprocess.

When the potatoes are ready, add them to the corn along with the tomato mixture, lime juice, and the remaining 1 tablespoon oil and 1/2 teaspoon salt. Toss until well mixed, then serve. ✳

# Curried Celery Root and Apple Salad

### SERVES 6

*Serve this pleasantly spicy salad as an accompaniment to roast turkey, baked ham, fried chicken, or cold cuts.*

#### FOR THE DRESSING

$^1/_4$ cup ($^1/_4$ oz/7 g) fresh parsley leaves

$^2/_3$ cup (5 fl oz/160 ml) light mayonnaise

3 tablespoons water

2 tablespoons lemon juice

1 tablespoon plus 1 teaspoon curry powder,
preferably Madras

#### FOR THE SALAD

1 large celery root (celeriac), peeled and quartered

2 Granny Smith apples or other tart green apples, unpeeled,
halved, and cored

$^1/_3$ cup (2 oz/60 g) dried currants

To make the dressing, using the metal blade, process the parsley until minced. Add the mayonnaise, water, lemon juice, and curry powder and process until smooth. Leave the dressing in the work bowl.

To make the salad, using the shredding disc, put the celery root quarters in the feed tube one at a time and process to shred. Then shred the apples the same way.

Transfer the salad to a bowl. Add the currants, stir until well mixed, and serve. ✴

39

# Two-Cranberry Chutney

### SERVES 12

3 cloves garlic

1-inch (2.5-cm) square peeled fresh ginger

1 large yellow onion, cut into 1-inch (2.5-cm) chunks

2 tablespoons vegetable oil

2 firm, ripe pears, peeled, cored, and cut into
1-inch (2.5-cm) chunks

$1/2$ cup (2 oz/60 g) dried cranberries

$1/4$ cup (2 fl oz/60 ml) distilled white vinegar

$1/4$ teaspoon cayenne pepper

2 teaspoons ground turmeric

3 cups (12 oz/375 g) fresh cranberries

$1/2$ cup (4 oz/125 g) plus 2 tablespoons sugar

41

Using the metal blade, turn the processor on and drop the garlic through the feed tube. Process until finely minced. Then drop in the ginger and process until finely minced. Add half of the onion chunks and pulse to chop coarsely.

In a large, nonstick sauté pan over medium heat, warm the vegetable oil. Add the contents of the work bowl. Immediately add the remaining onion chunks to the work bowl and pulse to chop coarsely. Add to the sauté pan. Cook, stirring often, until the onion has softened, about 7 minutes.

Meanwhile, add the pears to the work bowl and pulse to chop coarsely. Add the pears, dried cranberries, vinegar, cayenne pepper, turmeric, fresh cranberries, and sugar to the sauté pan. Stir well and bring to a simmer. Cook, stirring often, until the fresh cranberries just start to pop, 7–9 minutes.

Remove from the heat and transfer to a serving bowl. Let cool, then serve at room temperature. ✳

# Cucumber and Arugula Salad with Orange Vinaigrette

## SERVES 6

**FOR THE ORANGE VINAIGRETTE**

2 tablespoons finely shredded orange zest

3 large shallots

1-inch (2.5-cm) square peeled fresh ginger

1 cup (8 fl oz/250 ml) orange juice

1/3 cup (3 fl oz/80 ml) seasoned rice vinegar

1/3 cup (3 fl oz/80 ml) canola oil

1 teaspoon salt

ground pepper to taste

2 large English (hothouse) cucumbers, peeled, halved length-wise, and cut crosswise into 4-inch (10-cm) lengths

3 cups (3 oz/90 g) baby arugula leaves, stems removed, chilled

42

To make the vinaigrette, using the metal blade, process the zest, shallots, and ginger until finely minced. Add the orange juice, vinegar, oil, salt, and pepper. Process to mix. Leave the vinaigrette in the work bowl.

Using the slicing disc and working in batches, stand the cucumber pieces in the feed tube and process to slice. Transfer to a bowl and toss until well mixed. Taste and adjust the seasonings.

To serve, line a serving platter with the arugula and mound the cucumbers in the center. ✳

# Purée of Acorn Squash with Garlic

**SERVES 6–8**

*This simple purée tastes best the day it is cooked. It can, however, be made several hours ahead and kept at room temperature. To reheat, spoon into a baking dish, cover, and reheat in a pre-heated 350°F (180°C) oven until hot, about 30 minutes.*

3 tablespoons olive oil

several fresh thyme sprigs

4 acorn squashes, halved lengthwise and seeded

4 large cloves garlic, unpeeled

$1/4$ cup (2 oz/60 g) unsalted butter, at room temperature

$1/2$–2 tablespoons water

$2 1/2$ tablespoons honey

salt and ground pepper

Preheat an oven to 375°F (190°C).

43

Pour the oil into a jelly-roll (Swiss roll) pan or shallow roasting pan. Tilt the pan to spread the oil evenly over the surface, then scatter the thyme sprigs over the oil. Arrange the squash, cut sides down, over the thyme. Scatter the garlic cloves around the squash.

Bake until the squash is soft when pierced, about 1 hour. Remove from the oven and, when cool enough to handle, trim away and discard any scorched areas.

Fit the processor with the metal blade. Scoop the hot squash from its shell into the work bowl. Squeeze the soft garlic out of its peel into the work bowl. Add the butter, $1/2$ tablespoon water, and the honey and process until smooth, about 30 seconds. Add up to $1 1/2$ tablespoons additional water if the mixture is too thick. Season to taste with salt and pepper.

Transfer to a warmed serving bowl and serve immediately. ✳

# Zucchini Fritters with Fresh Tarragon

SERVES 4–6

*Tarragon enhances the flavor of both zucchini and potatoes. Serve these fritters with simply grilled or roasted meats, poultry, or fish. They can also be made smaller and served at room temperature with smoked salmon, dill, and sour cream as part of an hors d'oeuvre plate.*

2 tablespoons fresh tarragon leaves

I egg

$^{1}/_{4}$ cup (2 fl oz/60 ml) milk

6 tablespoons (I $^{1}/_{2}$ oz/45 g) all-purpose (plain) flour

I $^{1}/_{2}$ teaspoons baking powder

$^{1}/_{2}$ teaspoon salt

$^{1}/_{4}$ teaspoon ground nutmeg

$^{1}/_{4}$ teaspoon ground pepper

2 small zucchini (courgettes)

I Yukon gold potato, unpeeled, halved crosswise

about 2$^{1}/_{2}$ tablespoons canola oil

about 2$^{1}/_{2}$ tablespoons unsalted butter

Using the metal blade, combine the tarragon, egg, milk, flour, baking powder, salt, nutmeg, and pepper and process until mixed.

Using the shredding disc, stand the zucchini in the feed tube and process to shred. Place a potato half, cut side down, in the feed tube and process to shred. Repeat with the remaining potato half. Transfer to a bowl and toss until well mixed.

In a large, nonstick frying pan over medium heat, warm $^{1}/_{2}$ table-spoon each of the oil and butter. Working in batches, spoon the batter by tablespoonfuls into the pan, leaving about 1 inch (2.5 cm) around each fritter and spreading the batter out slightly with the back of a spoon. Cook, turning once, until golden brown on both sides, about 3 minutes on each side. Transfer to a platter and keep warm. Cook the remaining batter in the same way, adding more oil and butter to the pan as needed. Serve hot. ✳

**MAIN COURSES AND SAUCES**

# Beef Fillets with Curry and Cucumber Raita

### SERVES 6

#### FOR THE RAITA

⅓ cup (⅓ oz/10 g) each fresh mint leaves and dill leaves

2 large green (spring) onions, cut into pieces

2 English (hothouse) cucumbers, peeled and cut into 4-inch (10-cm) lengths

1½ cups (12 fl oz/375 ml) low-fat plain yogurt

½ cup (4 fl oz/125 ml) light sour cream

1½ teaspoons sugar

1 teaspoon salt

ground pepper to taste

#### FOR THE BEEF

6 filets mignons, each about 6 oz (185 g)

1½ tablespoons olive oil

1¼ teaspoons each salt and ground pepper

1 teaspoon ground cumin

#### FOR THE CURRY SAUCE

2 large cloves garlic

¾-inch (2-cm) square peeled fresh ginger

4 large shallots

1 large apple, unpeeled, halved, and cored

1 tablespoon vegetable oil

2 teaspoons each curry powder and sugar

1 teaspoon each ground cumin and ground turmeric

2 teaspoons all-purpose (plain) flour

3 cups (24 fl oz/750 ml) beef broth

¼ cup (1½ oz/45 g) dried currants

¼ cup (2 oz/60 g) tomato paste

To make the *raita,* using the metal blade, combine the mint, dill, and green onions and pulse until minced. Using the shredding disc, lay the cucumbers in the feed tube and process to shred. In a bowl, stir together the yogurt, sour cream, sugar, salt, and pepper. Add the contents of the work bowl and stir to mix. Cover and refrigerate for 3–6 hours.

To prepare the beef, rub the steaks on both sides with the olive oil. In a small dish, stir together the salt, pepper, and cumin. Sprinkle on both sides of the meat. Let stand for 2 hours.

Meanwhile, make the sauce: Using the metal blade, turn the processor on and drop the garlic through the feed tube. Process to mince. Then drop in the ginger and process to mince.

Using the slicing disk, stand the shallots in the feed tube and process to slice. Using the shredding disk, put the apple halves in the feed tube one at a time and process to shred.

In a large, nonstick frying pan over medium-high heat, warm the vegetable oil. Add the contents of the work bowl and the curry powder and stir well. Cook, stirring often, until the shallots have softened, about 5 minutes. Stir in the sugar, cumin, turmeric, and flour. Cook for 1 minute. Add the broth, currants, and tomato paste and stir well. Simmer, stirring often, until the sauce is the consistency of sour cream, about 10 minutes. Keep warm.

Meanwhile, prepare a medium-hot fire in a charcoal grill. Place the steaks on the grill rack and grill, turning once, about 4 minutes on each side for medium-rare, or until done to your liking. To test for doneness, cut into the center with a sharp knife. Transfer to a platter, cover loosely, and let rest for 10 minutes.

Taste and adjust the seasonings of the sauce, adding a little water if it is too thick. Slice the steaks. Spoon 2 tablespoons sauce onto each plate. Fan the beef slices over the sauce and drizzle the remaining sauce on top. Serve hot with the raita. ✳

49

# Spanish Potato Tortilla

### SERVES 4–6

$1/3$ cup ($1/3$ oz/10 g) fresh parsley leaves

2 large cloves garlic

1 large russet potato, about 10 oz (315 g),
peeled and halved lengthwise

4 tablespoons (2 fl oz/60 ml) olive oil

scant $3/4$ teaspoon salt

2 tablespoons water

2 small yellow onions, halved lengthwise

6 eggs

$1/2$ cup (4 fl oz/125 ml) heavy (double) cream

ground pepper to taste

Place a rack in the lower third of an oven; preheat to 350°F (180°C).

Using the metal blade, process the parsley leaves and garlic until finely minced. Set aside.

Using the slicing disc, place the potato halves in the feed tube and process to slice. In a large, nonstick frying pan over medium heat, warm 2 tablespoons of the olive oil. Add the potato slices and sprinkle with $1/4$ teaspoon of the salt. Cook, turning occasionally, for 10 minutes. Raise the heat to medium-high and add the water. Cook, turning twice, until tender, about 3 minutes. Set aside.

Using the slicing disc, place the onions in the feed tube and process to slice. In a heavy, ovenproof frying pan over medium-high heat, warm the remaining 2 tablespoons oil. Add the onions and cook, stirring often, until softened, about 4 minutes. Stir in the reserved garlic-parsley mixture.

Using the metal blade, pulse the eggs, cream, the remaining scant $1/2$ teaspoon salt, and the pepper just to mix. Pour evenly over the onions. Cook, moving the eggs to the center as they begin to set on the edges. When only half set, scatter the potato slices over the surface and press into the eggs.

Bake until set, puffed, and lightly browned, 15–18 minutes. Let rest for at least 10 minutes. Cut into wedges and serve. ☀

# Mediterranean Chicken with Leeks and Tomatoes

### SERVES 4

*Serve this dish for Sunday supper with rice, buttered noodles,
or mashed potatoes. Add a green salad, a crusty loaf of bread,
and a bowlful of berries for dessert.*

1/4 cup (1 1/2 oz/45 g) all-purpose (plain) flour

1 teaspoon dried thyme

1 teaspoon dried marjoram

1 teaspoon salt

ground pepper to taste

1 frying chicken, 3 1/2 lb (1.75 kg), cut into
serving pieces and skinned

2 large cloves garlic

2 leeks, white part only, cut in half lengthwise

1/2 lb (250 g) fresh mushrooms, stemmed

6 teaspoons olive oil

1 3/4 cups (10 1/2 oz/330 g) peeled and chopped
tomatoes (fresh or canned)

1/2 cup (4 fl oz/125 ml) dry white wine or dry vermouth

2 tablespoons tomato paste

pinch of sugar

1/2–3/4 cup (4–6 fl oz/125–180 ml) water

Position a rack in the lower third of an oven; preheat to 375°F (190°C).

Put the flour, thyme, marjoram, salt, and pepper in a lock-top
plastic bag. Shake to combine. Blot the chicken pieces dry. Trim
off the wing tips. Working in 2 batches, place the chicken in the
bag and shake to coat evenly. Shake off the excess flour mixture
and set the chicken pieces aside. Reserve the flour mixture.

Using the metal blade, turn the processor on and drop the garlic through the feed tube. Process until finely minced. Using the slicing disc, in batches, stand the leeks in the feed tube, fitting them snugly, and process to slice. Next, stand the mushrooms on their sides in the feed tube, fitting them snugly, and process to slice. Set aside.

In a large, nonstick frying pan over medium-high heat, warm 2 teaspoons of the olive oil. Add half of the chicken pieces and cook, turning once, until browned, about $2^1/_2$ minutes on each side. Transfer to a shallow baking dish large enough to hold all the chicken in a single layer. Wipe the pan clean, add 2 more teaspoons oil, and repeat with the remaining chicken.

Add the remaining 2 teaspoons oil to the pan and place over medium heat. Add the contents of the work bowl and cook, stirring often, until the leeks have softened, about 7 minutes. Sprinkle the reserved flour mixture over the vegetables and stir well. Cook, stirring, for 1 minute. Add the tomatoes, wine or vermouth, tomato paste, sugar, and $^1/_2$ cup (4 fl oz/125 ml) water, stir well, and bring to a boil. Pour evenly over the chicken. Cover the baking dish with aluminum foil.

Bake until the chicken is fork tender, about 1 hour. If the sauce seems too thick, add the remaining $^1/_4$ cup (2 fl oz/60 ml) water and shake the dish to mix it in. Serve hot directly from the dish. ✻

53

# Carrot, Brussels Sprout, and Red Pepper Stir-fry

### SERVES 6

4 large cloves garlic

two 1-inch (2.5-cm) squares peeled fresh ginger

2 small yellow onions

6 carrots, peeled and cut in half crosswise

1 lb (500 g) brussels sprouts, trimmed

2 large red bell peppers (capsicums), sides cut off in slabs, seeded, and slabs cut in half lengthwise

3 tablespoons peanut oil

1 teaspoon salt

4 teaspoons oyster sauce

4 teaspoons hoisin sauce

2 teaspoons seasoned rice vinegar

Using the metal blade, turn the processor on and drop the garlic, then the ginger, through the feed tube. Process until minced. Transfer to a dish.

Using the slicing disc, place the onions in the feed tube and process to slice. Lay 2 or 3 carrot pieces lengthwise in the feed tube and process to slice. Repeat until all are sliced. Transfer to a bowl. Stack half the brussels sprouts in the feed tube and process to slice. Repeat until all are sliced. Transfer to a separate bowl. Stand 2 or 3 red pepper slabs in the feed tube and process to slice. Repeat until all are sliced. Set aside.

In a large, nonstick wok over medium-high heat, warm the peanut oil. Add the garlic, ginger, onions, and carrots and toss and stir until the onions have softened, about $1^1/_2$ minutes. Add the brussels sprouts and salt and toss and stir until the cores are just tender, about 3 minutes. Add the bell pepper and toss and stir for 1 minute longer. Add the oyster sauce, hoisin sauce, and rice vinegar and mix well. Serve hot. ✳

# Chunky Vegetable Chili

## SERVES 8

*Coarsely chopped kidney beans give substance to this basic chili mixture. As with most recipes for chili, this one is best made at least a day ahead, so the flavors have a chance to develop fully. If you like, substitute carrots and mushrooms for the butternut squash and zucchini. Serve with shredded cheddar cheese, thinly sliced green (spring) onions, sour cream, and fresh cilantro (fresh coriander) leaves for adding at the table.*

2 large cloves garlic

1 small jalapeño chile, seeded, if desired

1 large yellow onion, cut into 1-inch (2.5-cm) chunks

1 tablespoon vegetable oil

2 cans (15 oz/470 g each) kidney beans,
rinsed and well drained

1 can (28 oz/875 g) whole tomatoes with juice

1 can (6 oz/185 g) tomato paste

2 1/2–3 1/2 cups (20–28 fl oz/625–875 ml) vegetable broth

2 tablespoons chili powder

2 teaspoons ground cumin

1 teaspoon dried oregano

1 small butternut squash, about 1 1/2 lb (750 g),
halved lengthwise, seeded, peeled, and cut into
1-inch (2.5-cm) cubes

2 zucchini (courgettes), cut into 1-inch (2.5-cm) cubes

1 cup (6 oz/185 g) fresh or frozen corn kernels

1 cup (5 oz/155 g) frozen petit peas

salt to taste

Using the metal blade, turn the processor on and drop the garlic through the feed tube. Process until finely minced. Then drop in the chile and process until minced. Turn off the processor. Put half the onion chunks in the work bowl and pulse to chop coarsely.

In a heavy, nonaluminum soup pot over medium-high heat, warm the vegetable oil. Add the contents of the work bowl. Immediately add the remaining onion chunks to the work bowl and pulse to chop coarsely. Add to the pot. Cook uncovered, stirring often, until the onion has softened, about 4 minutes.

Meanwhile, add 1 can of beans to the work bowl and pulse to chop coarsely. Add them to the pot. Add the tomatoes and their liquid to the work bowl and purée until smooth. Add them to the pot along with the remaining can of whole beans, the tomato paste, $2^1/_2$ cups (20 fl oz/625 ml) of the vegetable broth, the chili powder, cumin, and oregano. Stir well. Bring to a boil over medium-high heat. Reduce the heat to medium-low and simmer, stirring often, until slightly thickened, about 10 minutes.

Working in batches, add the butternut squash and zucchini to the work bowl and pulse to chop coarsely. Add the chopped squashes to the pot and simmer, stirring often, until the vegetables are tender, about 20 minutes. Add the corn and peas and cook for 4 minutes longer. Season with salt. Taste and adjust the seasonings.

Serve at once, or let cool, cover, and refrigerate for up to 3 days. Before serving, reheat gently, adding the remaining 1 cup (8 fl oz/ 250 ml) broth and/or water if the mixture is too thick. ✳

57

# Penne with Broccoli and Pesto

### SERVES 6

*Classic Italian pesto is easiest made in a processor. You can make the pesto ahead, cover it with a thin layer of olive oil, and store it in the refrigerator or freezer.*

**FOR THE PESTO**

2-oz (60-g) piece Parmesan cheese, at room temperature

2-oz (60-g) piece pecorino cheese, at room temperature

2 large cloves garlic

1/4 cup (1 1/2 oz/45 g) pine nuts

1 cup (1 1/2 oz/45 g) firmly packed basil leaves

1 cup (1 1/2 oz/45 g) firmly packed baby spinach leaves

ground pepper to taste

1/4 cup (2 fl oz/60 ml) olive oil, plus oil for drizzling

1/2 lb (250 g) penne

2 1/2 cups (5 oz/155 g) broccoli florets

salt and ground pepper to taste

6 lemon wedges

To make the pesto, using the metal blade, combine the Parmesan and pecorino cheeses and pulse to break up, then process to mince. Add the garlic cloves, pine nuts, basil, spinach, and pepper. Process to mince. With the processor on, slowly pour the 1/4 cup (2 fl oz/60 ml) olive oil through the feed tube and process until smooth. Transfer to a large, shallow serving bowl.

Bring a large pot of salted water to a boil. Add the penne and cook until al dente (tender but firm to the bite), about 12 minutes. About 2 minutes before the pasta is ready, add the broccoli.

Reserve some of the cooking water, then drain the pasta and broccoli and transfer to the pesto. Toss gently to mix, adding cooking water if the sauce is too thick to coat the pasta evenly. Season with salt and pepper. Serve immediately with the lemon wedges. ✳

# Vietnamese-Style Stir-Fry of Beef and Vegetables

### SERVES 4

*Here, it is essential to have all the ingredients processed and ready, as the cooking is very quick. Serve the stir-fry with steamed rice.*

**FOR THE MARINADE**

1 clove garlic

3/4-inch (2-cm) cube peeled fresh ginger

3 tablespoons hoisin sauce

2 tablespoons vegetable oil

1 tablespoon water

2 teaspoons Asian sesame oil

2 teaspoons soy sauce

1 lb (500 g) flank steak, trimmed of excess fat, cut lengthwise into thirds, and then thinly sliced across the grain

1 cup (1 oz/30 g) loosely packed fresh cilantro (fresh coriander) sprigs, including stems

3 large cloves garlic

1 small yellow onion

12 baby carrots

1 small zucchini (courgette)

1/2 jicama, peeled and halved

1/4 small head green cabbage, cored and cut in half

1 1/2 tablespoons vegetable oil

3 oz (90 g) small fresh shiitake mushrooms, brushed clean and stems trimmed

1/4 lb (125 g) snow peas (mangetouts)

1/2 teaspoon sugar

1/2 teaspoon salt

red pepper flakes to taste

To make the marinade, using the metal blade, turn the processor on and drop the garlic, then the ginger, through the feed tube. Process until finely minced. Transfer to a large, heavy-duty lock-top plastic bag and add the hoisin sauce, vegetable oil, water, sesame oil, and soy sauce. Add the beef, seal the bag, and turn to coat the beef evenly. Let stand at room temperature for 30 minutes.

Meanwhile, using the metal blade (do not wash the work bowl), process the cilantro sprigs until finely minced. Set aside.

Still using the metal blade, turn the processor on and drop the garlic through the feed tube. Process until finely minced.

Using the slicing disc, stand the onion in the feed tube and process to slice. Group 5 baby carrots together and stand them in the feed tube. Wedge in 1 more. Top with a second layer. Process to slice. Set aside. Stand the zucchini in the feed tube and process to slice. Set aside. Stand the jicama halves in the feed tube, cut sides down, and process to slice. Stack the slices together, stand them in the feed tube, and process to slice into matchsticks. Set aside. Stand the cabbage wedges in the feed tube, cut sides down, and process to slice. Set aside.

In a large, nonstick wok or deep sauté pan over medium-high heat, stir and toss the beef and the marinade until just cooked through, about 3 minutes. Set aside. Return the wok or pan to medium-high heat and warm the vegetable oil. Add the garlic, onion, carrots, and mushrooms. Toss and stir until heated through but still crisp, about 2 minutes. Add the zucchini, jicama, snow peas, sugar, salt, and red pepper flakes. Toss and stir until heated through but still crisp, about 2 minutes longer.

Return the beef to the pan along with the cilantro and cabbage. Toss and stir until just heated through, 1–2 minutes. Taste and adjust the seasonings.

Immediately transfer to a warmed platter and serve at once. ✳

# Grilled Lamb Patties with Mint

### SERVES 4

*Fresh mint adds the defining flavor to these lamb patties.
For perfect texture, use the pulse motion to chop the ingredients
in two batches. Serve the patties in warm pita bread rounds with
mayonnaise, sliced tomato, green leaf lettuce, and a condiment
made from mixing together sliced cucumbers, crumbled feta
cheese, and Kalamata olives with red wine vinegar.*

1 lb (500 g) lamb from the leg, trimmed of fat and
cut into 1-inch (2.5-cm) cubes

1 small yellow onion, quartered

1 cup (1 oz/30 g) loosely packed fresh mint leaves

1 tablespoon olive oil

generous $^1/_2$ teaspoon salt, plus salt to taste

$^1/_2$ teaspoon ground pepper, plus pepper to taste

63

Prepare a medium-hot fire in a charcoal grill. Put a few chunks
of mesquite in water to cover. Oil the grill rack.

Using the metal blade, combine half of the lamb, onion, mint,
olive oil, and the $^1/_2$ teaspoon each salt and pepper. Pulse to chop.
Set aside. Repeat with the other half of the ingredients. Return
the first batch to the work bowl. Pulse 2 times to combine the
halves. Carefully remove the metal blade. Gently shape the mixture
into 4 equal patties. (At this point, the patties can be covered
with plastic wrap and refrigerated for several hours before grilling.)
Sprinkle lightly with salt and pepper.

Toss the mesquite chunks onto the coals. Place the patties on
the grill rack and grill, turning once, until browned on both sides,
about 6 minutes total for medium-rare or until done to your
liking. To test for doneness, insert the point of a sharp paring
knife into the center.

Transfer to individual plates and serve hot. ✳

# Baked Tubetti with Vegetables and Cheese

### SERVES 6

*Tubetti, a narrow macaroni shape, or pennette, a small version of the popular penne, work especially well in this delicious do-ahead dish, but other small pasta can be substituted. Serve with any simply grilled meat, seafood, or poultry.*

1 red bell pepper (capsicum)

10 oz (315 g) tubetti

3 tablespoons olive oil

$^3/_4$-lb (375-g) piece part-skim mozzarella cheese or Monterey jack cheese, chilled and halved

3-oz (90-g) piece Parmesan cheese, rind removed, at room temperature

2 large cloves garlic

1 large shallot

$^1/_2$ lb (250 g) small fresh mushrooms, brushed clean and halved if large

$^1/_3$ cup ($^1/_3$ oz/10 g) fresh basil leaves

1 small zucchini (courgette), cut crosswise into 3 equal pieces

1 small eggplant (aubergine), peeled and cut into 1-inch (2.5-cm) cubes

$^1/_2$ teaspoon fennel seeds

$^1/_2$ teaspoon salt

red pepper flakes to taste

1 jar (26 oz/815 g) spicy pasta sauce

Preheat a broiler (griller). Cut off the bottom and sides of the bell pepper in flat slabs. Discard the top and any seeds. Place the slabs, cut sides down, on an aluminum foil–lined baking sheet. Broil (grill) about 6 inches (15 cm) from the heat until the skins blacken and blister. Remove from the broiler and wrap the pepper loosely in the foil lining. When cool enough to handle, peel away the skin and set the pepper aside.

Bring a large pot three-fourths full of salted water to a boil. Add the pasta and cook until nearly al dente (tender but firm to the bite), about 10 minutes. Drain, place in a bowl, add 1 tablespoon of the olive oil, and toss to mix well. Set aside. Preheat an oven to 350°F (180°C). Butter a 2$^1$/$_2$-qt (2.5-l) baking dish.

Using the shredding disc, process the cheeses to shred. Transfer to a bowl and toss until mixed. Set aside.

Using the metal blade, turn the processor on and drop the garlic, then the shallot, through the feed tube. Process until both are minced. Turn off the processor. Add the mushrooms and basil. Pulse to chop coarsely.

In a large frying pan over medium heat, warm the remaining 2 tablespoons olive oil. Add the mushrooms to the pan and cook, stirring occasionally.

Meanwhile, still using the metal blade, pulse the roasted pepper and zucchini together to chop coarsely. Add to the pan and continue to cook. Pulse the eggplant to chop coarsely and add to the pan along with the fennel seeds, salt, and red pepper flakes. Raise the heat to medium-high and stir and toss until all the vegetables are just tender, about 3 minutes. Stir in the pasta sauce. Taste and adjust the seasonings; the mixture should be highly seasoned. Transfer to a large bowl. Add the cooked pasta and stir well.

65

Layer half of the pasta mixture in the prepared baking dish. Sprinkle with half of the cheese mixture. Top with the remaining pasta, spreading evenly. Sprinkle with the remaining cheese. Cover loosely with aluminum foil.

Bake for 35 minutes. Remove the foil and continue to bake until the edges are browned and sizzling, about 15 minutes longer. Let rest for 10 minutes before serving. ✳

# Chicken Fajitas with Guacamole

## SERVES 4

*Canned chipotle chiles in adobo sauce can be found in ethnic sections of well-stocked food stores and in Latin American markets. Serve the fajitas family style with the chicken and vegetables mounded on a platter and warm tortillas, guacamole, and sour cream in separate dishes surrounding the platter.*

### FOR THE MARINADE

2 large cloves garlic

1 ½ cups (12 fl oz/375 ml) unsweetened pineapple juice

3 tablespoons canola oil

1 ½ tablespoons honey

1 tablespoon puréed canned chipotle chile in adobo sauce

1 tablespoon chili powder

1 ¼ teaspoons salt

2 large skinless, boneless chicken breast halves,
cut into long strips ½ inch (12 mm) wide

1 large sweet onion such as Vidalia, halved

1 large green bell pepper (capsicum)

### FOR THE GUACAMOLE

1 green (spring) onion, white part only

1 small jalapeño chile, seeded

1 ripe Hass avocado, halved, pitted, and cut into cubes

1 small tomato, seeded and quartered

2–3 teaspoons lime juice

scant ⅛ teaspoon salt

2 tablespoons canola oil

3 tablespoons fresh cilantro (fresh coriander) leaves

sour cream

8 flour tortillas, warmed

To make the marinade, using the metal blade, turn the processor on and drop the garlic through the feed tube. Process until finely minced. Turn the processor off. Add the pineapple juice, canola oil, honey, chipotle chile, chili powder, and salt and pulse to mix. Set aside.

Place the chicken in a heavy-duty lock-top plastic bag, add 1 cup (8 fl oz/250 ml) of the marinade, and seal the bag. Turn to coat the chicken evenly and refrigerate for at least 30 minutes or for up to 3 hours.

Using the slicing disc (do not wash the work bowl), stand an onion half, cut side down, in the feed tube and process to slice. Repeat with the other onion half. Cut the sides off the green pepper in 4 or 5 large slabs. Cut them in half crosswise. Using the slicing disc, stand the slabs in the feed tube and process to slice. Transfer the vegetables to a bowl. Wipe out the work bowl with paper towels.

To make the guacamole, using the metal blade, turn the processor on and drop the onion, then the chile, through the feed tube. Process until both are finely minced. Turn off the processor. Scrape down the work bowl. Add the avocado, tomato, and 2 teaspoons of the lime juice. Pulse to chop coarsely, so the guacamole has some texture. Taste and adjust with more lime juice and salt.

In a large, nonstick frying pan over medium-high heat, warm the canola oil. Add the vegetables and cook, stirring often, until softened, about 4 minutes. Add 1 cup (8 fl oz/250 ml) of the remaining marinade. Simmer uncovered, stirring often, until most of the marinade has evaporated, about 8 minutes. Remove from the heat and keep warm.

In a medium frying pan over medium-high heat, cook the chicken with its marinade, stirring often, until opaque throughout, about 3 minutes.

To serve, transfer the vegetables to a warmed platter and arrange the chicken on top. Garnish with the cilantro leaves. Serve immediately with the guacamole, sour cream, and tortillas. ✳

# Citrus Sauté of Shrimp and Fennel

### SERVES 6

*If you wish, substitute 1½ pounds (750 g) bay or
sea scallops for the shrimp. Serve on pappardelle or fettuccine
tossed with butter and snipped chives.*

2 large cloves garlic

2 small fennel bulbs, trimmed, quartered
lengthwise, and cored

2 tablespoons unsalted butter

1 tablespoon finely shredded orange zest

³/₄ cup (6 fl oz/180 ml) fresh orange juice

½ cup (4 fl oz/125 ml) water

½ teaspoon salt

¼ teaspoon red pepper flakes, or to taste

2 lb (1 kg) large shrimp (prawns), peeled with
tail segments intact and deveined

3 green (spring) onions, thinly sliced

Using the metal blade, turn the processor on and drop the garlic
through the feed tube. Process until finely minced. Using the
slicing disc, stand the fennel quarters in the feed tube and process to slice.

In a large, nonstick frying pan over medium-high heat, melt the
butter. Add the garlic, fennel, and orange zest and cook, stirring
often, until the fennel is heated through but still firm, about
4 minutes. Add the orange juice, water, salt, and red pepper flakes
and simmer, uncovered, until the liquid is reduced by half, about
6 minutes.

Add the shrimp and continue to cook, stirring often, until they
just turn opaque, 3–4 minutes. Stir in the green onions.

Transfer to a warmed serving dish and serve at once. ✳

# Pan-Sautéed Duck Breasts with Plum-Cranberry Marmalade

### SERVES 4

*The sweet-tart marmalade complements these well-seasoned duck breasts. Serve with wild rice.*

**FOR THE MARMALADE**

1 clove garlic

1 small yellow onion

1 tablespoon vegetable oil

3 large, firm plums, halved and pitted

1/4 cup (1 oz/30 g) dried cranberries

1/4 cup (2 fl oz/60 ml) balsamic vinegar

2/3–1 cup (5–8 fl oz/160–240 ml) low-sodium chicken broth

1–2 teaspoons sugar

1/2 teaspoon salt

ground pepper to taste

**FOR THE DUCK BREASTS**

2 whole boneless duck breasts, split in half, trimmed of excess fat, and skin scored

3/4 teaspoon salt

ground pepper to taste

To make the marmalade, using the metal blade, turn the processor on and drop the garlic through the feed tube. Process until minced.

Using the slicing disc, stand the onion in the feed tube and process to slice.

In a nonstick frying pan over medium heat, warm the oil. Add the garlic and onion and cook, stirring often, until softened, about 4 minutes.

Meanwhile, using the slicing disc, stand the plum halves in the feed tube and process to slice. Add to the pan and cook until softened, about 3 minutes. Stir in the cranberries, vinegar, $^2/_3$ cup (5 fl oz/160 ml) of the broth, 1 teaspoon of the sugar, the salt, and the pepper. Simmer until thickened, about 4 minutes, adding as much of the remaining $^1/_3$ cup (3 fl oz/80 ml) stock as needed to keep the mixture from drying out. Taste and add the remaining 1 teaspoon sugar if the mixture is too tart. (The marmalade can be made 2 days ahead, covered, and refrigerated. Before serving, reheat gently, adding a little water if it is too thick.)

To cook the duck breasts, heat a heavy frying pan over medium-high heat until hot. Season the breasts with the salt and pepper. Place them, skin sides down, in the hot pan and cook until well browned and the fat has rendered, about 5 minutes. Drain off all but a small amount of the fat. Turn the breasts over and continue to cook until browned on the second side, about 3 minutes longer for medium-rare. Transfer to a warmed platter and tent with aluminum foil. Let rest for 10 minutes.

71

To serve, remove the skin from the breasts and cut across the grain into thin slices. Arrange each sliced breast attractively on a warmed individual plate. Pour the duck juices that accumulated in the platter into the marmalade. Stir well, reheat gently, and taste and adjust the seasonings. Spoon the warm marmalade around each duck breast, reserving a small dollop for the top. Serve at once. ✳

SWEET ENDINGS

# Fresh Peach Pie

**SERVES 8**

**FOR THE CRUST**

3 cups (15 oz/470 g) all-purpose (plain) flour

2 tablespoons sugar

1 teaspoon salt

$1/2$ cup (4 oz/125 g) solid vegetable shortening,
chilled and cut into 4 pieces

$1/2$ cup (4 oz/125 g) chilled unsalted butter, cut into 8 pieces

$1/2$ cup (4 fl oz/125 ml) plus 2 tablespoons ice water

**FOR THE FILLING**

10 peaches, peeled, halved, and pitted

1 tablespoon lemon juice

1 tablespoon vanilla extract (essence)

$3/4$–1 cup (6–8 oz/185–250 g) sugar

3 tablespoons quick-cooking tapioca

3 tablespoons all-purpose (plain) flour

1 teaspoon ground cinnamon

pinch of salt

2 tablespoons unsalted butter, cut into small pieces

**FOR THE GLAZE**

1 tablespoon heavy (double) cream or milk

2 teaspoons sugar

$1/4$ teaspoon ground cinnamon

vanilla ice cream (optional)

To make the crust, using the metal blade, combine the flour, sugar, and salt and process to mix. Distribute the shortening and butter evenly over the flour mixture. Pulse to form a coarse, uneven mixture. Spoon the ice water evenly over the flour mixture. Pulse just until a few clumps form. Do not overprocess.

Transfer the dough to a plastic bag and compress it into a ball. Remove from the bag and divide into 2 portions, one twice as large as the other. Flatten each portion into a disc; flecks of shortening and butter should be visible. Wrap separately in plastic wrap and freeze for 15 minutes.

Preheat an oven to 450°F (230°C).

On a lightly floured work surface, roll out the larger dough disc (keep the other disk refrigerated) into a 12-inch (30-cm) round. Drape it over the rolling pin and carefully transfer it to a deep 9-inch (23-cm) pie dish. Gently ease the pastry into the dish, pressing it into the bottom and sides. Roll out the smaller dough disc into a 10-inch (25-cm) round. Transfer to a baking sheet and refrigerate until needed.

To make the peach filling, using the slicing disc, stand the peach halves in the feed tube, two at a time, and process to slice. Repeat until all the peaches are sliced. You should have 8–9 cups (4 lb/ 2 kg). Transfer the slices with their juice to a large bowl. Add the lemon juice and vanilla and toss well. In a small bowl, stir together 3/4 cup (6 oz/185 g) sugar (or more if the peaches are not very sweet), the tapioca, flour, cinnamon, and salt. Add to the peaches and toss until evenly coated. Let stand for 20 minutes, then trans- fer the filling to the pie dish, gently mounding it in the center. Dot the surface with the butter.

Transfer the refrigerated pastry to the top of the pie, carefully centering it. Trim the edges, leaving a 1/2-inch (12-mm) overhang. Tuck the overhang under to seal it tightly, then form a decorative edge with the tines of a fork or your fingers.

To make the glaze, brush the entire top crust with the cream or milk. In a small dish, stir together the sugar and cinnamon. Sprinkle evenly over the surface. Cut a few steam vents in the top.

Place the dish on a baking sheet and bake for 15 minutes. Reduce the oven temperature to 400°F (200°C) and bake until the crust is golden brown and the juices are bubbling, 45–55 minutes. If the edges begin to become too brown, protect them with strips of aluminum foil. Transfer to a wire rack to cool until the juices are thickened, about 3 hours. The pie is best served slightly warm the day it is made. (If it cools completely, gently reheat in a 300°F/ 150°C oven until heated through, about 15 minutes.) Cut into wedges and top each serving with ice cream, if desired. ✳

# Espresso Granita

*A refreshing conclusion to dinner, a granita can be easily frozen and then processed only once just before serving, rather than the repeated stirring many recipes require. Serve it plain or topped with lightly whipped sweetened cream and sprinkled with cocoa or ground cinnamon.*

2 cups (16 fl oz/500 ml) hot brewed espresso coffee

¹/₂ cup (4 oz/125 g) sugar

Combine the coffee and sugar in a 4-cup (32–fl oz/1-l) heatproof measuring pitcher and stir until the sugar dissolves. Refrigerate until cool.

Divide the coffee mixture between 2 standard ice-cube trays. Freeze until solid, at least 4 hours or for as long as a week.

Before processing, let the trays rest at room temperature until the cubes just begin to loosen around the edges, about 8 minutes. Then, using the metal blade, pulse 6 espresso cubes until finely minced. Transfer the granita to a metal bowl and store in the freezer while processing the remaining batches.

To serve, stir the granita with a fork and divide among chilled glasses. Serve immediately. ✳

# Apple Pandowdy

### SERVES 6–8

*Pandowdy, a classic New England recipe, is a deep-dish fruit dessert topped with a crust. The crust is baked until it starts to brown, and then it is cut into small squares— "dowdied"—and pressed down into the apples. The dessert is returned to the oven until well browned. Although typically made with biscuit dough, here pastry dough is used, which holds up better to the juices during baking.*

### FOR THE PASTRY DOUGH

1 1/2 cups (7 1/2 oz/235 g) all-purpose (plain) flour

1 tablespoon sugar

1/2 teaspoon salt

1/2 cup (4 oz/125 g) solid vegetable shortening, chilled, cut into 4 pieces

5 tablespoons (2 1/2 fl oz/75 ml) ice water

### FOR THE APPLE FILLING

5 large Granny Smith apples, peeled, halved, and cored

2 teaspoons vanilla extract (essence)

2/3 cup (5 oz/155 g) sugar

2 tablespoons all-purpose (plain) flour

2 teaspoons ground cinnamon

pinch of salt

3 tablespoons water

2 tablespoons unsalted butter, cut into small bits

1 teaspoon milk or heavy (double) cream

1 1/2 teaspoons sugar

vanilla ice cream (optional)

To make the pastry dough, using the metal blade, combine the flour, sugar, and salt and process to mix. Add the shortening. Pulse to make a coarse, uneven mixture. Spoon the ice water evenly over the flour mixture. Pulse just until a few clumps form. Do not overprocess. Transfer the dough to a plastic bag, compress it into a ball, and flatten it into a disc. Small flecks of shortening should be visible. Freeze for 15 minutes.

Preheat an oven to 400°F (200°C). Butter a 9-inch pie dish or a shallow 1½-qt (1.5-l) baking dish.

To make the apple filling, using the slicing disc, stand the apple halves in the feed tube one at a time and process to slice. Transfer the slices to a large bowl. Add the vanilla and toss well. In a small dish, combine the sugar, flour, cinnamon, and salt. Add to the apples and toss to coat. Arrange the apple slices in the prepared dish. Drizzle evenly with the water. Dot the apples with the butter pieces.

On a lightly floured work surface, roll out the dough into an 11-inch (28-cm) round. Transfer to the prepared dish and trim flush with the dish rim. Brush the pastry with the milk or cream. Sprinkle with the sugar. Cut steam vents in the top.

Place the dish on the baking sheet and bake until the pastry is lightly browned, about 30 minutes. Reduce the temperature to 350°F (180°C). Remove the dish from the oven. Cut the pastry into 1-inch (2.5-cm) squares. Using the back of a spoon, gently press the squares into the apples. Continue to bake until deeply browned and the juices are bubbling, about 45 minutes longer. Remove from the oven and let cool on a rack for at least 2 hours. Serve warm with ice cream, if desired. ✳

# Sliced Strawberries with Citrus Sugar

SERVES 4

*Citrus sugar imparts a flavor boost to fresh fruit and
berry desserts, hot or iced tea, lemonade, and yogurt toppings.
It can be stored in an airtight container in the refrigerator
for up to 2 weeks.*

1 tablespoon finely shredded orange zest

1 tablespoon finely shredded lemon zest

$^2/_3$ cup (5 oz/155 g) sugar

1 $^1/_2$ pints (12 oz/375 g) strawberries, hulled

2 tablespoons lemon juice

3 tablespoons vodka or orange juice

Using the metal blade, combine the orange and lemon zests and
the sugar. Process until finely minced. Set aside.

Using the slicing disc, fill the feed tube with strawberries and
process to slice. Repeat until all the strawberries are sliced.
Transfer to a bowl.

Add $^1/_2$ cup (4 oz/125 g) of the citrus sugar, the lemon juice, and
the vodka or orange juice to the strawberries and toss gently to
mix. Taste and add more citrus sugar if needed. Cover and refrigerate for at least 1 hour or for up to 4 hours.

To serve, toss gently and serve chilled in small bowls. ✳

# Maple Walnut Cheesecake

SERVES 12

*Making cheesecake becomes a simple task when both crust and filling are prepared in a food processor. Walnuts, bourbon, and maple flavoring combine to give this version a mellow flavor.*

### FOR THE CRUST

1/3 cup (1 1/2 oz/45 g) walnuts

50 vanilla wafers (7 oz/220 g)

2 tablespoons light brown sugar

pinch of salt

6 tablespoons (3 oz/90 g) unsalted butter, melted

### FOR THE FILLING

1/2 cup (2 oz/60 g) walnuts

3 eggs

1/2 cup (4 oz/125 g) granulated sugar

3/4 lb (375 g) cream cheese, at room temperature, cut into 6 equal pieces

3/4 cup (6 fl oz/180 ml) heavy (double) cream

2 tablespoons all-purpose (plain) flour

1 tablespoon bourbon whiskey

1 1/2 teaspoons vanilla extract (essence)

1 1/2 teaspoons maple flavoring

pinch of salt

5 large walnut halves

Preheat an oven to 225°F (110°C). Butter a 9-inch (23-cm) springform pan.

To make the crust, using the metal blade, combine the walnuts, vanilla wafers, brown sugar, and salt and process until finely minced. Pour the melted butter evenly over the crumbs. Pulse until clumped together, then process continuously until uniformly crumbled. Transfer the crumbs to the center of the prepared pan. Using a plastic bag as a mitten, press some of the crumbs about 1 inch (2.5 cm) up the sides of the pan. Spread the remaining crumbs evenly over the bottom. Press firmly into place. Set aside.

To make the filling, first wipe the work bowl and the blade with paper towels. Using the metal blade, pulse the walnuts to chop coarsely. Set aside.

Add the eggs and sugar and process until light yellow and foamy, stopping once to scrape down the sides of the work bowl. Add the cream cheese and pulse to break up, then process until smooth. Add the cream, flour, bourbon, vanilla, maple flavoring, and salt. Process until well mixed. Spoon the chopped walnuts evenly over the batter. Pulse to mix in the nuts. Pour the batter over the crust. Place the pan on a baking sheet.

Bake until the cheesecake does not jiggle in the center when the pan is gently shaken, about 1½ hours. Turn off the oven and leave the cake in the closed oven for 35 minutes. Then transfer to a rack and let cool. Cover and refrigerate for at least 6 hours or for up to 2 days before serving.

Garnish with the walnut halves and let stand for about 1 hour at room temperature before serving. ✳

83

# Mango Sorbet

**SERVES 4 OR 5**

*Nowhere is the magic of the food processor more evident than when it is used to transform small cubes of frozen fresh fruit into a smooth sorbet.*

1 ½ large, ripe mangoes, peeled, pitted, and cut into 1-inch (2.5-cm) cubes

½ cup (4 oz/125 g) sugar

1 tablespoon finely shredded orange zest

3–4 tablespoons lime juice

Arrange the mango cubes in a single layer on a baking sheet. Freeze until solid, about 1 hour.

Completely thaw about ³/₄ cup (4¹/₂ oz/140 g) of the mango cubes at room temperature. Set aside. Once thawed, remove the remaining mango from the freezer and thaw only until the tip of a sharp knife can be inserted into a cube; the fruit should still be very firm.

Using the metal blade, combine the frozen mango with the sugar and orange zest and pulse to break up. Then process until finely minced, stopping once to scrape down the sides of the work bowl. Scatter the thawed mango evenly over the frozen minced fruit, and add 3 tablespoons of the lime juice. Process until very smooth and the sugar has dissolved, about 1¹/₂ minutes. Taste and add the remaining 1 tablespoon lime juice, if needed.

Transfer to a freezer container and freeze briefly for a firm consistency. If frozen for more than 1 day, it may be necessary to reprocess the sorbet to make it smooth once again.

Scoop into chilled bowls and serve. ✳

# Spiced Pear Cake

### SERVES 12–16

*The food processor makes mixing this old-fashioned bundt cake a snap. First, it sifts together the dry ingredients, then blends in the eggs and molasses. The pears, which must be almost inedibly hard, are mixed in at the end.*

### FOR THE CAKE

3 cups (12 oz/375 g) cake (soft-wheat) flour

1 teaspoon baking soda (bicarbonate of soda)

1 teaspoon salt

1 1/2 teaspoons ground cinnamon

1-inch (2.5-cm) square peeled fresh ginger

1 cup (8 fl oz/250 ml) vegetable oil

1 2/3 cups (13 oz/410 g) granulated sugar

3 eggs

2 teaspoons vanilla extract (essence)

3 tablespoons dark molasses

2 large, very firm pears, peeled, cored, and cut into 3/4-inch (2-cm) chunks

### FOR THE TOPPING

1/4 cup (2 oz/60 g) unsalted butter

1/2 cup (3 1/2 oz/105 g) firmly packed light brown sugar

2 tablespoons heavy (double) cream

2 teaspoons confectioners' (icing) sugar

86

Preheat an oven to 350°F (180°C). Generously butter a nonstick 10-inch (25-cm) bundt pan. Lightly dust with flour, tapping out the excess.

To make the cake, using the metal blade, combine the flour, baking soda, salt, and cinnamon and process briefly to "sift." Transfer to a large bowl and set aside. Turn the processor on and drop the ginger through the feed tube. Process until finely minced. Scrape down the sides of the work bowl and add the oil, granulated sugar, eggs, vanilla, and molasses. Process until smooth.

Spoon the reserved flour mixture evenly over the top of the egg mixture. Pulse just to combine most of the flour. (Do not over-process. The surface flour will be mixed in with the pears.) Transfer the batter to the large bowl. Stir in the pears, then spoon the batter into the prepared pan.

Bake until a toothpick inserted into the center comes out clean, about 1 hour. Let cool in the pan on a rack for about 5 minutes. Invert the cake onto the rack and lift off the pan. Place the rack on a sheet of aluminum foil.

While the cake is cooling, make the topping: In a small saucepan over low heat, combine the butter, brown sugar, and cream. Heat until the butter melts. Stir to mix well.

Brush the warm cake with the topping, reapplying any that drips onto the foil. Let cool until warm. Just before serving, using a fine-mesh sieve, sift the confectioners' sugar evenly over the cake. ✳

# Pecan Finger Cookies

### MAKES ABOUT 100 COOKIES

*These crisp, rich mouthfuls are irresistible in the cookie jar and great enhancements to simple fruit and sorbet desserts.*

1 egg, separated

1 cup (7 oz/220 g) firmly packed light brown sugar

1 cup (8 oz/250 g) unsalted butter,
at room temperature, cut into 4 equal pieces

2 teaspoons vanilla extract (essence)

$\frac{1}{8}$ teaspoon salt

2 cups (10 oz/315 g) all-purpose (plain) flour

1 cup (4 oz/125 g) pecan pieces

Using the metal blade, process the egg white until frothy. Transfer to a small bowl. Add the egg yolk, brown sugar, butter, vanilla, and salt to the work bowl (it is not necessary to wash the work bowl) and process until smooth and fluffy, stopping once to scrape down the sides of the bowl. Spoon the flour evenly over the batter, then spoon the pecans over the flour. Pulse to combine, then process just until the dough forms a ball.

Transfer the dough to a large sheet of plastic wrap. Using the wrap as a glove, shape the dough into a rectangle about 7 by 11 inches (18 by 28 cm) and $\frac{1}{2}$ inch (12 mm) thick. Freeze until firm, about 30 minutes.

Preheat an oven to 350°F (180°C). Cut the chilled dough in half lengthwise to form 2 long rectangles, then cut crosswise into slices $\frac{1}{4}$ inch (6 mm) thick. Working in batches, arrange on 2 ungreased baking sheets, spacing the slices about 1 inch (2.5 cm) apart. Lightly brush each with the reserved egg white.

Bake until browned at the edges, 18–20 minutes. Let cool for 5 minutes on the baking sheets, then transfer to a rack to cool completely. Repeat with the remaining dough and egg white. ✳

89

# Bittersweet Torte with Hot Fudge Sauce

### SERVES 12–16

*The food processor eliminates the need to melt the chocolate for both the torte and the sauce. For the torte, process the bread crumbs first in the clean work bowl, then measure out what you need. Unlike many tortes, this one cuts easily into perfect thin slices.*

**FOR THE TORTE**

1 slice high-quality white bread, crusts trimmed, torn into pieces

1 1/3 cups (5 1/2 oz/170 g) walnuts

8 oz (250 g) bittersweet chocolate, broken into pieces

2 teaspoons baking powder

pinch of salt

6 tablespoons (3 oz/90 g) unsalted butter, at room temperature, cut into 3 equal pieces

3/4 cup (6 oz/185 g) granulated sugar

5 eggs, separated

2 teaspoons vanilla extract (essence)

**FOR THE FUDGE SAUCE**

3 tablespoons unsalted butter, at room temperature

1/4 cup (2 fl oz/60 ml) heavy (double) cream

1/4 cup (2 fl oz/60 ml) whole or low-fat milk

4 oz (125 g) bittersweet chocolate, broken into pieces

1/2 cup (4 oz/125 g) granulated sugar

1 teaspoon instant-espresso powder

pinch of salt

1 teaspoon baking powder

1 tablespoon vanilla extract (essence)

2 teaspoons confectioners' (icing) sugar

coffee ice cream and/or vanilla ice cream

90

Preheat an oven to 350°F (180°C). Butter the bottom and sides of a 9-inch (23-cm) springform pan and line the bottom with parchment (baking) paper or aluminum foil cut to fit exactly. Butter the parchment or foil.

To make the torte, using the metal blade, process the bread until finely crumbled, about 5 seconds. Measure the crumbs and return $^1/_4$ cup ($^1/_2$ oz/15 g) to the work bowl. Freeze the remainder for another use. Add the walnuts, chocolate, baking powder, and salt to the work bowl and pulse to break up the chocolate. Then process continuously until finely and uniformly minced, about 20 seconds. Transfer the chocolate mixture to a large bowl.

Using the metal blade, combine the butter, sugar, egg yolks, and vanilla. Process until creamy, about 1 minute. Add to the chocolate mixture. Using a wooden spoon, combine to form a batter.

In a bowl, using an electric mixer, beat the egg whites until they just hold their shape. Stir one-fourth of the egg whites into the batter to lighten it. Using a rubber spatula, fold in the remaining whites just until no white streaks remain. Transfer the batter to the prepared pan.

Bake until a toothpick inserted into the center comes out just moist but not wet, 35–38 minutes. Remove from the oven and let cool in the pan on a rack. It is okay if the torte sinks a bit. Once the torte is cool, remove the pan sides and slide the torte onto a serving plate. Drape your hands with plastic wrap and gently compress the sides to even out the surface.

To make the fudge sauce, in a small saucepan, combine the butter, cream, and milk. Place over low heat until the butter melts. Stir well and keep hot.

Using the metal blade, combine the chocolate, granulated sugar, espresso powder, and salt. Pulse about 5 times to break up the chocolate, then process continuously until finely minced. With the processor still on, slowly pour the hot mixture through the feed tube and process until the chocolate is melted. Add the baking powder and vanilla. Process just until mixed. You should have about $1^1/_2$ cups (12 fl oz/375 ml). Transfer to a warmed pitcher.

Just before serving, using a fine-mesh sieve, sift the confectioners' sugar over the top of the cake. Cut into thin wedges and serve with ice cream and a drizzle of the hot fudge sauce. ✳

# Lemon Tart with Pecan Crust

**SERVES 8–10**

*The nut crust is a delicious favorite. It is easily and quickly made in the processor, and you don't need to roll it out or line the shell with parchment (baking) paper and weights as it bakes.*

### FOR THE PECAN CRUST

1 cup (4 oz/125 g) pecan pieces

1 1/4 cups (6 1/2 oz/200 g) all-purpose (plain) flour

1/3 cup (3 oz/90 g) sugar

1/2 teaspoon salt

1/2 cup (4 oz/125 g) plus 2 tablespoons unsalted butter, at room temperature, cut into 8 pieces

1 egg, lightly beaten

1 tablespoon vanilla extract (essence)

### FOR THE LEMON GARNISH AND FILLING

1 small, firm lemon, ends trimmed flat

1 tablespoon finely grated lemon zest

1 1/3 cups (11 oz/340 g) sugar

4 eggs

1/2 cup (4 oz/125 g) unsalted butter, melted and cooled

1/2 cup (4 fl oz/125 ml) lemon juice

1/4 cup (2 fl oz/60 ml) sour cream

### FOR THE TOPPING

2 teaspoons sugar

1 teaspoon vanilla extract (essence)

3 cups (24 fl oz/750 ml) chilled heavy (double) cream

Preheat an oven to 350°F (180°C).

To make the crust, spread the pecans on a baking sheet and toast in the oven until lightly golden and fragrant, 5–7 minutes. Let cool completely.

Using the metal blade, combine the flour, cooled pecans, sugar, and salt and process until the pecans are finely minced. Distribute the butter, egg, and vanilla evenly over the flour. Pulse until mixed and clumps start to form. Transfer the dough to an 11-inch (28-cm) tart pan with a removable bottom. Press evenly into the bottom and sides of the pan. Freeze for 15 minutes. Place the pastry-lined pan on a baking sheet and bake until lightly browned on the edges, about 25 minutes.

Meanwhile, make the lemon garnish and filling: Using the slicing disc (wipe out the work bowl with paper towels), stand the lemon in the feed tube and process to slice. Wrap in plastic wrap and refrigerate until needed.

Using the metal blade (do not wash the work bowl), combine the lemon zest and sugar and process until the zest is finely minced and the mixture is fragrant. Add the eggs and process until very smooth and fluffy. With the processor on, pour the butter and lemon juice through the feed tube. Turn the processor off. Add the sour cream. Pulse until smooth. Pour into the hot crust.

Bake until the filling is set, about 25 minutes. Set aside to cool completely, then cover and refrigerate to chill well.

To make the topping, using the metal blade (and a clean work bowl), put the sugar and vanilla in the work bowl. Turn the processor on. Pour the cream through the feed tube and process until thick.

Spread a thin layer of the cream over the chilled tart. Spoon the remaining cream into a pastry bag fitted with a star tip and make rosettes around the edge. Remove the seeds from the reserved lemon slices, make 1 cut from the center to the edge of each slice, and twist the cut edges in opposite directions. Garnish the tart with the twisted lemon slices. Serve chilled, cut into wedges. ✳

# INDEX